Chug the

Story by Jenny Giles
Illustrated by Chantal Stewart

2

Chug the tractor
helped on the farm.
He went up and down the hills.
Chug!   *Chug!*   *Chug!*

One day he said,
"I can't get up
the big hill today.
I am too old."

He went slowly back
to the tractor shed.
Ch . . . ch . . . chug.   *Ch* . . . ch . . . chug.

The next day
a big yellow tractor
came into the shed.
He looked down at Chug.
"I am the new tractor," he said.
"I have come to help on the farm.
You are too old.
You are going to the **dump**."

Chug went away
on the back of the farmer's truck.
"Oh!" he cried. "Oh, help!"

"I am too old.
No one likes me, now.
I am going to the dump."

On and on down the road
went Chug.

He went all the way to town
on the back of the truck.

12

The truck went into a little park.
Some men came to help Chug
get down.

"This is not the **dump**!"
said Chug.
"This is a beautiful park!"

14

The next day,
the children who played
in the little park
ran to see Chug.

"Look at the new tractor!"
they shouted.
"It's for us to play on!"

"The children like me," cried Chug.
"I am not too old, after all."